The Blue Canoe
of Longing

Poems

Margot Farrington

DOS MADRES

2019

DOS MADRES PRESS INC.

P.O.Box 294, Loveland, Ohio 45140

www.dosmadres.com   editor@dosmadres.com

Dos Madres is dedicated to the belief that the small press is essential to the vitality of contemporary literature as a carrier of the new voice, as well as the older, sometimes forgotten voices of the past. And in an ever more virtual world, to the creation of fine books pleasing to the eye and hand.

Dos Madres is named in honor of Vera Murphy and Libbie Hughes, the "Dos Madres" whose contributions have made this press possible.

Dos Madres Press, Inc. is an Ohio Not For Profit Corporation and a 501 (c) (3) qualified public charity. Contributions are tax deductible.

Executive Editor: Robert J. Murphy

Illustration & Book Design: Elizabeth H. Murphy
www.illusionstudios.net
Cover Photo: Margot Farrington,
"Voyage With Wave And White Bird"
Author Photo: Tony Martin

Typeset in Adobe Garamond Pro & Papyrus
ISBN 978-1-948017-60-2
Library of Congress Control Number: 2019947336

First Edition

ACKNOWLEDGEMENTS

I thank the editors of magazines and anthologies who first published these poems. I'm also grateful to those who make the Platte Clove Artist-in-Residence Program possible, where compressed time but long-sustained memories inspired certain poems for this book.

American Society: What Poets See: "Foreclosure"

Arabesques Review (Algeria): "The House Speaks Of Layers" (originally published as "Continuum")

A Women's Thing: "Ant On Granite Seacoast," "Lullaby For Sights And Sounds On The Island"

Ekphrasis: "Yakshi With A Love Letter In Her Hand"

Fourth River: "The Mouse"

Innisfree Poetry Journal: "Highland"

Like Light: 25 Years of Poetry & Prose by Bright Hill Poets And Writers: "Counterweight," "Giorgio"

Southword (Ireland): "Aftermath"

The Second Word Thursdays Anthology: "Sloppy And Mephisto," "Rake (Among Fallen Leaves)"

Poetry Wales: "Gravedigger"

For Tony

Table of Contents

Part II   Reappearances

Part III   Crossroads

I. Appetites

Conception In May

I must've known May was the only month I
stood a chance to be conceived. People's coats
came off, the lindens lifted bicolored bouquets
while the mockingbird married ecstasy
on the highest aerial of the neighborhood.
Laundry flirted along the lines—a pair of panties flew off
while the rest swelled with innuendo. A handprint
preserved in cement beckoned me on.
Smokers sensed my drift by way of their exhalations.
In the subway, a rat ran along
with a piece of paper held in its mouth as all who saw it
pointed and laughed without a trace of fright.
Outside the air was buxom, fragrant where
flowers ruled, their scent elusive among
taxis who drove in pursuit, fast then slow.
A couple kissed at an intersection, the synchronized
streetlights greened. Pollen blew goldenly over
exhaust. I sensed an opening and
made my move.

Yakshi With A Love Letter In Her Hand

Necklace pouring over
melon breasts, the
sway of her girt thighs,
both ornamented arms forward,
her navel a hypnotist's eye.
Both ornamented arms forward,
one hand hacked away,
and the hand that remains,
open.
Limp from her
heat, the letter lies
across her palm.
Resting.
Loosely secured by a
chipped thumb,
requiring of us
surrender
and absolving disgrace.
She moves even the obtuse,
the numb, to read
what the body says,
be smitten by the
ripple she lives within.
Mysteries pass
over the planes of her
sandstone face.
Blank to begin, her
eyes change,
begin to
apprise.

The Hummingbird, The Zinnias

The hummingbird. The zinnias.
The hummingbird. The zinnias.
The hum. The hum-um-ummmm.
The zin. The zin, zin - zoom with
coordinates locked.
Bliss is a kiss, is a zin-zin.
Color me, says hummingbird,
honey me for the trip.

There's a time - drip in the nectar clock,
no stopwatch for the seconds.
Talk of Time's wingèd! No chariot,
though somewhere within
body's boom & thrum, a fly-wheel
turns,
incandescent.

What can you catch of the hummer,
slow spectator? Sipping your
coffee or tea. Brazilian or zin-zin-cinnamon.
Your tongue saying Zanzibar.
Mind blown by the
ruby and emerald needle honing in,
sewing a seam in cloth
you're included in, Big Flower.

Then needle says Flash,
puts in reverse zipper,
opening the sky and your heart.

Wine

So I had a glass or two.

Soon I was swaying like a cobra,
not to music others could hear
yet
music hypnotic ruled,
and the charmer
though invisible
beguiled everywhere:

in the silky bannister
leading upstairs and
faint friction of sheets, in the
swoon and plunge,
the dissolve that gaped in secret,
shaking us, shaking
then smoothing,
folding us into a nap.

A single note
announced our waking,
later you told me
how I tasted. Wine, the wine
still poured
via the nearby stream
sounding our windows, filling
the room to the rim.
The charmer by this time was
wood thrush whose notes
summoned a crush of
currant, hints of
blackberry too,
flavoring the finish.

Hunger

I'd not yet eaten, but walked where the
feast was spread. The first course offered
wild rose in a pasture's corner, slice of
path cutting uphill to walls of stacked stone,
ferns I brushed by, ferns I picked to
press to my face, inhaling the prehistoric.
I partook of one gadabout cloud, its belly tickled on
tree-tips, and blueberries picked while the
towhee whistled to his darling, while
lichen's wedding veil went on
                               spreading over stones.

Second course: stumps rearing from a vernal pool
(beasts rampant and regardant) while underfoot on
sodden leaves an ember crept on legs: red eft
whose fictive heat forged a glowing arrow.
Where should it point but to a feather? This I
caressed into shape, then let its falling spiral
write unwritten thoughts:
                     these were for everyone, for none.

Third course was the fox unseen but longed for,
hawthorns in first blush, heaven locked in the look of
hayfields alternating with new corn
sprung late but thriving after rain,

and somewhere beyond—plaintive—
                     came the killdeer's cry.

I was insatiable and devoured
every bit of the morning. The acres a full
banquet, and my appetite no surprise.

To The Hummingbird
Trapped In Ace Hardware

Brazen as plumber's chain, the sheen of
your breast. Gloss of barbecue hoods reflects
your flight. Earlier on, says the checkout girl, you
hovered, tried to reorient. You buzzed the
power tool display and spectrum of spray paint.
What. An. Odd. Garden.
You could make no sense of it, and
consigned your escape to speed.

Open-mouthed, the faucets. See the focused
squint of screws. Tapes fail to measure
mystery sky. Lumens strobe; you strobe.
Hammers fall through your heartbeat.
Scissors can't snip you from the scene, nor glue
paste you back in the bee balm: there was a
red irresistible, and how you
guarded it, little zealot! That patrolled
patch where nectars blazed. Welding gloves
and fire extinguishers hang helpless beneath
your orbit. They are watching your fuel tank
empty, your price rise.

What hope of a doorway when
you will not come down?
Soon you'll wed the speed of light,
become your own hallucinogen, where the
siren flower flares and the honey of midnight
drips. Wind you barely felt blew you
off course. Wind and the bright

chrysanthemums tiered by the
automatic doors. One of us let you in, but
none can net a meteorite. Watching you lap
the store recalls how we coveted your speed,
and the many ways we've attained it.
How in the frenzy we sustained, we
bred the fierce changes.

The Return

Think back—if you think life's short—to the prow of a canoe
cleaving water while you paddled and
your double did the same.
Drops wept from the wooden blade and healed into her
face. In unison you stroked as the mists of morning scrolled.

Where on the opposite shore did you eat your sandwich,
tip canteen? When did you sprawl against wooden ribs,
fall asleep? And waking, find the afternoon ablaze,
but the shade kindly. You lay pinned to a gaze,
pulse transferred to

Dragonfly. Big cerulean stitch, he was basted to your
jeans, where he bid you look him in the eyes and
be lost in the millennia. Meanwhile, he
divined you and the weave of faded denim,
and he could have held you there forever
though he chose to let you go.

Here he hovers in the mind's shimmer, or seeks you along
the brook. Seamless, he trolls the hours, drawing
summers together: this one and that one
melting until you are achingly young, and he tells you
that somewhere you still sleep,
and your reflection sings from the lake.

Elderflower In Bloom

White umbels plentiful, you signal: time for
winemaking. Should blossoms missed
for that purpose persist, berries
progress towards banquet.
The hungry waxwing comes, the
finch and thrush. The catbird
mimicking between bites. The sparrow
subtle in the lull. Human hands come picking,
intent on jam or syrup. Dark as caviar,
your wealth. Some, foraging as summer wanes,

call you black lilac, when great with bounty
you curtsy to the breeze, your branches
asway, easily broken. You're fashion from start to finish:
wear first the topping lace you trade for
beads of green, then purple, and at last like a
dowager don those of jet.

At present, you wait, white umbels opened out.
White umbrellas? first raindrops query.
White umbrels? they question.
Umbels! they cry, pell-mell.
Umbel-l-l-llll! crashes Thunder. I say, tumble down your
whites to the hue of my sound you borrow to
color your berries. Um-umbel! Thunder stutters,
by this tumbrel I drive through the cobbled sky
I command you: give over your whites;
it is mid-July. By August you must offer darkness to
do me honor. Therefore this rain—my prompt
from purpled sky. Hurry! Be fruitful.

Morning Tea

Again the cup kisses saucer.
As if this domestic click

Conjures touch with others,
As if water drawn from the tap

Seeks return to the well,
A doe sets foot on the road,

Turning to check and nuzzle her
Fawn, urging her precious to pay

Heed while I wait with them and
Raise my cup.   I too sense the invisible

Gate and would pass through with
Them, striving to hear my heart in

Cadence with their hooves. They're
Abreast of the apple tree, part without

Sound the willows. Pure pattern,
Hard to discern—but why let that deter?

Why not focus and why not shatter into
Spots alchemized to silver (fawn dapple,

Brook, sun-disc reflected in my cup)
As each of us deeply drinks.

Sharing Mussels

When the sea comes to Giorgio
in the guise of blue-black butterflies
he opens their wings with
white wine, lemon, and garlic.
We might well be gulls—nothing
but cries and swoops for more
amidst clacking of shells on plates.
Chanced upon pieces of grit
work a burin where teeth meet,
but aside from these sounds there's
only silence soft as kelp.

Fresh, fresh from the sea an hour ago.
What will we say when at last we speak?
Won't our words be hinged and winged,
bearing tinges of mother of pearl?
Sean offers up the last one.
Boris gestures, helpless.
Linda laughs. Laughs again
as I lay slow claim.

Moored to our bench, we want nothing.
But here comes Giorgio with bread.
We dip slices in the broth. The bounty of
Sally and Sarah has made us sleepy
with surfeit, feast that blue-eyed Sally
and Sarah (whose every glance is green),
dug from marine mud.
Each of their motions mimed a wave,
and the sea had nodded,
the sea had said Yes.

Giorgio

It was said of Giorgio he knew every egg in his kitchen.
Soon we discovered he could turn beef into butter.
When we'd arrived he bid us to carefully listen;
No one must touch the refrigerator or the wine—

we would have plenty, served and poured by his hand.
More than anything, said Giorgio, he hated waste.
In wartime his people had eaten rat, pigeon, and
cat. Who'd ruined the oven? How to compensate? He

aced the lack by using the outdoor grill. What did he grill?
Oh, luna moth, stone, cormorant. Okay, he didn't, but
don't think he wasn't capable. Our chef could instill
polenta with Puccini. Savoring red pepper soup, our

tongues held a note by Callas. Lord and servant
stirred together. Pride sandwiched humility.
Ladle in hand, our benevolent lion waited. Sent
us to table with laden plates. Fifty-five years of

cooking, forty-three of marriage. Quite an equation.
"I never rush in my life for anything," he grinned,
"except—(the grin grew wide) for my wife." Lunch
over, he sat on a Maine deck to take the Venetian sun.

Counterweight

Taken. His pair of bantam roosters, bright and
trim. Frontline soldiers who sought to protect
their hens. Small hearts stout, they tightened,
sprang to spur. Outmatched. One would expect

the usual outcome. Fox killed both. Two tassels hung
from her jaws. Two bronze bells swung, tolling
a voiceless knell. Robbie told his wife. She was stung
by his loss and pictured the fox at ease, lolling

in a meadow, gorged and content. Shoot it, she said.
Not knowing what he had seen: gaunt old vixen,
torn-eared, grizzled hairs overtaking the red.
Staunch. She'd noted and planned for chicken:

two kits were waiting. Likely her last go-round
of offspring. (*Defeat*, his dead bantams said).
I must. He heard the vixen utter without sound.
(*Kill that fox*, said the ghosts of farmers long dead).

Robbie thought it over. Avenge his two by killing three?
He'd set up the incubator. Each hand cupped an egg.
He gentled them into hollows. His verdict came easily
then: mercy for the fluent one never created to beg

nor to know of pardon. Pardon was Robbie's province.
Sharpening, silvering, the old mother would persist
as long as rough gods bid before her fade into the mists
the island made. Regardless, hatchings and crowings since.

Ant On Seaside Granite

The vast expanse.
Noontime rock you
hotfoot over.
Harried by the hunt.
Casting back
on your own tracks,
or upon
those sought.
Scenting someone.
Surrendering to hesitation.

Little One, where do you
wander, Little One, where do you
roam, the sea sings as you head for the
edge. That's not the way to the library,
not the path to the farmer's market. What
waits among the wrack? Among
whelk traffic and periwinkle parking?
Tiny Ebony, where is home?

Bald, this granite. Daunting.
Yet you
progress,
free from the knowledge of
foundation,
threshold,
lintel,
statue and
gravestone.
How public

you are, how urgent.
How private whenever you halt.
Any moment, you'll disappear,
my Speck among flecks.
Quick—tell me who
you make the journey for.

Ant Found In An Empty Crab Shell

I never expected to find you engaged in a
race against reason. Or do you race time?
Sweep of the second hand has you. Beneath
my shadow, you slow not a whit. That I block the
sun on your fifteenth lap seems not to faze you.
You round curves without crash: the dimpled
surface provides traction. You're breaking a
record, giving your all inside this amphitheater.

Then, the iPhone in your head begins
to ring. You slow, but keep course. Wife or husband
talks. Where are you, by the way, and how long
will it take you to get home? Have you remembered to
mail the bills? I see you falter; your mandibles
drop, you close them with effort.
Gaining the upswell of an edge, you clamber over.
Do I imagine you nearly fall? That you
totter off, diminished?

I turn your racetrack over, exposing dull red.
Dreamer, here lies rough terrain, a realm of
dead volcanoes, and look—embedded at the
border, a pair of eyes the sun baked white.

Dilettante Encounters Claw

Oh, but you're handsome, propped against a pebble.
Sun has scoured you albino. How modern you
look, like a Frank chair or an Arp sculpture.

Oddly modern, and—Wow—with what ease you seize me!
Thought you were ossified.

My—ouch!—apologies. Was (God!) wrong?
My watering eyes perceive how Day dazzles.

Tingling in ghost-grasp. What? The sea is pouring into my ears.
Dead, did you say? Which one of us?

Is this love or just a crush?

I'm a fool? But you'll let me live, if I
promise to *really* live?

I thought I *was* living. I'm not? You mean, I wasn't?
Your grip is *so* strong.
Thrilling, I must say. I love to be thrilled.

Lullaby For Sights And Sounds
On The Island

Lighthouse, no. Buoy, yes.
Blear, smear the coastal satin.
Hush gull and soothe seal
should wing, should head appear.

Pines darken, black sharpen hue but
not edge. Boat be known by
hull of sky. Currents, come home.
Sand wear down small to smallest:
wild gains by grain.

Thrush, anneal song to heaven.
Star flower foam. Fog
take heed and tide keep secret.
Ocean pretend lake. Salt moon
and store by day. Breathe
dimmed blaze. Tauten sail for
night watch. Midnight will tailor.

Sleeping In Pearls

Deep in the filigree of the catch, the wee hook went
awry. Was it revenge? I hadn't worn those pearls in
years. I strategized before the mirror, cursing in whispers.

Your deep and even breathing sounded from our
bed. I thought of oysters then, and of origins. I
went to the window, my hands about my neck,

naked but for the necklace. The moon,
sporting risqué clouds, studied me.
Lunacy, she inferred, to go on trying. Wear them,

she advised. They break? Get them re-strung.
Give in, let morning solve what tonight
cannot. I crept to join you then, careful not to

wake you. Your heat welcome, the sheet
stretched taut and chill behind me. Rolling pearls
between my fingers, I fretted about choking

but their smoothness counseled sleep. The night grew
easeful as I warmed, and I loosened. Only
silk thread kept the luminous planets aligned.

They had been plucked from depths like those I felt
pull upon me now. I drew you to me,
and the necklace held.

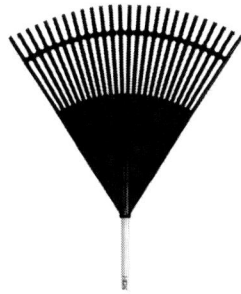

II. Reappearances

The Wallpaper Suite

I. Preparing To Scrape

Sponge in hand, I plunge it in the bucket of warm
water with vinegar added. Taking this wall by storm,

I joke to myself, because no lightning changes
happen; it's slow work. Hateful elsewhere, it's strange

that here I find it engrossing. The paper's skin
turns umber under the wetting. I stroke the water in,

swimmer of circular moves, landlocked in a closet.
The original hue was probably golden ochre. Doesn't

time conspire to darken or bleach? Look how little
flowers in the pattern--linked by deftly scribbled

stems, color up against the tender paper's dark.
Water's brought them to life; they nearly sparkle

from the unexpected soaking my freakish Spring
provides. Blindly intent, full of innate daring,

she turns them lush ivory. They're sugar - petaled, fresh
with the sorcery of birth. Motionless, I stand enmeshed

in the garden of once only, I for whom they bloom,
innocent of their erasure. Powerless, these doomed

flowers, yet they wield power who soon will be extinct:
packed solid with ghosts, pressing me towards the brink

that lurks everywhere, waiting to be overstepped.
Where, for an amber moment, I am preserved and kept.

II. Wallpaper (A History)

You never know what histories wait beneath
the skin of an old house. Risky to expose sheaves

of beribboned wheat, bound like the waists of women.
To tear ivy tendrils and pale lattice, rip autumn

scenes among whose scattered leaves bronzed
pheasants disdain to put their feet, avoiding fronds of

ferns, treading the blanks between as though
misstep might trigger chaos. Scraping's a slow

revelation; out come these chance bits
that startle: an azure fragment, scarlet - tipped,

or scrap purely Pompeian, terra cotta with black
that hooks you out of your era backwards—back to

Herculaneum. There, Vesuvius broods: that volcano
recalls she burnt you to ash and wants you to know.

III. Aftermath

Even as I scrape to get the paper off, its flowers
persist: compendium of a century's hours.

I've gotten down to bare wood; still they remain.
Something in the stencil ink that made them stains,

transfers to boards a luminous silver. As if snails, in their
glide - treks over this surface, became ensnared

in the baroque, and could only pursue travel
mapping curves of pistil and stamen, sepal and petal.

Nailed here are the planks the paper hid, their span
encompassing fifteen, sixteen inches. What sort of man

felled those trees, planed them smooth? Hammered
them home to make this box? That sound heard

by a woman planning her future; she'd already
picked the pattern. Picture this closet new, steady

delight of those early days of open then close:
lit entries, dark exits. She loved what she'd chosen

for the closet: infant among the family of rooms,
enclosing, locket - like, a specific smell. Entombed

briefly, I scent, like some hound of the supernatural,
all that was bustling flesh and blood, radiantly spectral.

IV. Tripping

Under the blade the paper molts in long strips.
Just this section to go, then you'll call it quits

and go get a sandwich. Funny how the confines
of a closet work, hallucinogenic, expanding the mind

from where you stand cornered, so to speak.
The repetitive movement you make completes

your altered state. You travel places you haven't gone
in years. A Russian couple's farm, where from the pond

the grandfather came, staff in hand, herding geese.
Wine cellar in the Berkshires where hands smelling of anise

raised your face, then clasped you round your back,
his anise-flavored tongue touching yours, the near-blackout

of pleasure. What about the depths from which crabs
came (magically soundless) at Barnegat, as with elaborate

care you drew the weighted fish head up? Blue Evinrude,
blades lifted from the bay, now mute. Banked clouds alluded

to the squall approaching. You'd scoot beneath a dock,
hear boards above take blindly their tattoos, and locked

within opacity, sat thrilled.   Ah. The spent days remain
loyal in their way. Some with supreme cunning abstain

from any change. They know they're perfect, the reason
you've chosen dark on a summer's day. Treason

is always self-protection. This closet holds the vestige of a forest.
And you? You're the fugitive hiding here to avoid arrest.

Scraping, you never stop scraping while you trip. The work
moves to and fro, decade - slicing till something jerks

you out of it. What? Where are you? Your arm aches;
you're reprocessing, piecing visual bits in the awakening.

The door's ajar. Window - blaze beyond. August of infinite sky.
Wood observes you through knots as brown, as

large as horses' eyes.

The House Speaks Of Layers

She ran out of the willow pattern after papering east,
north and west, and finished with blowsy roses,
trellised on stripes. Necessity's mismatch, they
climb a bedroom's south wall. Whether she cried or
took the shortage in stride, no one living now can say.

Later occupants used paint without bothering to
strip. That's a shortcut time rewards with
puckers and splits. Children mapped new worlds
by discovering the old. They peeled and tore. Thus,
the 19th century debuts once more. Medallions
eye you in the study, filigree winds along the hall.
Look all you want, but call the realtor.   Soon you'll
shuffle plans and paint chips.

She ran out of the willow pattern after papering east,
north, and west. She cried or took the shortage
in stride, only I, the house, can say.

One day your shade, pale against Prussian blue,
will startle the seventh owner—the breath she draws
yours: a share that chills you both.
She might cry. Might take it in stride. This realm
belongs to me; the outcome mine alone to decide.

Demolition Of A 19th Century Wall

When the plaster came down, I saw
how the horses had served once more

and envisioned a van closing doors on a
load that shook as hooves hammered.

Dust of the stable yard wafted
farewell and prayer. Lather broke out

when men reopened the van. Light spoke
with the tailgate's crash, but ahead of

sight, of sound, came smell redolent with
one story. Each horse inhaled the odds,

grew still a moment. From an entrance
blew the chill devoid of season.

Holding a broken chunk, I felt of the blend:
slaked lime and slaughter held it together.

Like breast of mourning dove, the color
mingled mauve and old rose, and within,

aswirl in the mix, thousands of hairs.
Countless, they were, yet each ensnared

my eye into counting, till press of the
herd in solidarity exerted such strength

a shudder ran through me floor to ceiling,
and traveled every wall's length.

During The Renovation

Out of rubble I swept for bagging, tumbled
the bone. Distinct from broken lathe and

plaster, pale upon planks laid a century
plus fifty ago, came a wizened assertion

I held between thumb and forefinger while
speculating. Chicken, I started with that,

but the bone, quickening, said no. I
cannot say how it livened in my hand,

yet small as it was it besieged me with
suggestion, and as I turned it, trying to decide

what beast it came from, it began to glide
more easily, to power the turns itself. Could

that be? How had it wound up entombed
in the wall? Were there more I'd missed? Soon

I'd toss it, let it rejoin debris, but the bone
cautioned, said *wait*. Murmured. Murder?

I grew still. Had someone—? What it inferred
was monstrous. False. The room, stripped

down to lathe, looked grim. Weird, the way the
doorjambs warped a fraction more,   swayed

by what the bone implied. The half-blind
window, obscured by filth and a board

nailed over the lower pane, squinted.
Marooned in fancies, I squatted there and

listened to insinuations. How alone
I was. If only I could laugh. The quality of

the air had changed. Something sepulchral,
damp, seemed to have wiped the place

of familiarity. And yet I'd known that room
thirty years, stored archives—half my life in

there. How to explain the shift? Perhaps when
walls were exposed the balance changed. Lathe is

bone of a sort. A sympathy born between structure
and material? Or was it a tear in time's weave,

the hour tainted, too far gone to confess:
It's only a bone. You've plenty yourself to bare,

and will, in the cruelty of calendars, come to that.
Get on with your work. Throw this bone away.

The Beauty And Terror Of Good-bye

My dearest,
I must
take leave of you
depart, flee, fly
swiftly
as hunters
kingsmen, robbers,
police, conspirators pursue

before sunrise reddens
I need to be
fording the river,
hiding deep in a ditch,
galloping somebody's fabled grey,
catching the next   very next
taxi, train, plane.

Don't weep, rant,
despair, fall prey to
madness, give in
nor give up, I assure you
I'll resurface, appear out of the
mist, make known my
presence by a sign.

Before I go, I want to say
how beautiful you are in this
birch grove, cellar, hotel room,
hayloft, whorehouse,
it takes every bit of my strength

my every screaming fiber
to split, scram, go, exit,
take a powder,

how can I?   Make me, or we'll
both die—look what I've done,
look what we've done
and yet you've never looked
so lovely

wait for me
at the old sawmill
by the railroad tracks
at the intersection of Tanner and Reynolds
wait under the El, tarry by the
Blue Diamond
or the oak twice struck
by lightning let me look at you let me
look at you
let me have a minute before

sirens,
cathedral bells, midnight's implacable owl,
worked-up mob calling for
blood but never mind
let me look at you   let me fix you firmly
before I go
and if

I should never see you again
don't—I know this plan will work—

but if it doesn't   come visit
if you have knowledge of where I lie
lay a flower against earth
pour bourbon upon the unmarked
stone   discover or
intuit where my bones reside
and kiss me now
kiss me, let go of me let go.
I loved you,
whatever they say
I love you and I'll
see you again
or if I don't
goodbye, adieu,
farewell, so long,
remember the day we met
and hey—
stay sweet.

Rake (Among Fallen Leaves)

Under my motions,
the rake speaks
in rising voices, stiff sea roar,
yet collects such silence in the mind.
I hear my precious seconds,
in a chamber carved
behind a waterfall. It has
always existed. Always.
    How long have I existed?

Damply I stand,
transfixed; I've taken root in the chamber's stone floor.
One ear's gone deaf. Completely.
The other's painfully pressed
against scenes engraved in a
great bronze door.

Gravedigger

You think a hole hasn't got its hoard of secrets?
What hasn't come up as I went down, my shovel
extension of my arm? Not just at graves
but elsewhere. In my garden. The woods.
Some place by the railroad tracks.
Something strong say dig, I dig. Someone
unseen to me say: there.

Doll's head. Horse shoe. Marble. Key escutcheon.
Watch crystal. Cup handle.
Once, oh my, locket with portrait.

What they mean? What you
want them to mean. How do you view life?

Doll's head: cherish your kids.
Horse shoe: luck calls to luck.
Marble stands for charity to children of others.
Key escutcheon? Should be plain: don't peep
on the privates sides of people.
Watch crystal—if smashed—the fall of arrogance.
If intact, I take to mean the shield of infinity.
Cup handle speaks of need: the thirst for home.
Locket with portrait? (I know not many
ever found one of these).
I opened, found her pale, dark-eyed and
dark haired. Her dress the color of
chicory: a flower not meant to be picked.
And she means memory circles. Fierce,
like a hellhound. Or like a stone thrown far—
how much it says in still waters.

Love Poem To A Maple Leaf
In Ouleout Creek

Trapped by the stem, you stay, though
water forbids stillness—you must move,
pleasured by that caress.

Soft from immersion, tender as suede, your
 pale underside faces sky to court my

downward gaze. You alone make
me tremble to watch my minutes, surrendered

over a lip of stone as each is touched
and taken. The tally mounts, you grow wilder,
more sensual in water than ever you were in wind.

No mercy. Here lies the test of our constancy.
You waver, flip to reveal your
covert side. Red, of course, unforgettable red—

current quick as knives cuts your tether.
In seconds I spot you downstream.

Foreclosure

That wasn't the place we bought, but think
how long it's mortgaged memory. That
seller striving mightily to please.
Dining room, he said, but we could alter
that. Second bedroom—perhaps we'd want
to make it work space? Tidy, I recall. House
situated in a hollow. The claim
of the '49 Chalmers tractor
and the dog's unusual name.

Immaculate barn. We'd have cut the
umbilicus three generations long:
been first not to farm this place. Those
bales destined for mulch or nothing at all, the pile
hauled out: ziggurat sinking into muck.
Would clean Holsteins help to sell? His were
buffed dominos, watching from their stanchions.

Jubal. That was the dog's name.
Again, he hits the end of his chain. I hear the
choke closing on windpipe, squeezing frenzy to a
whisper. His dance nearly a gallows waltz, and
his prayer a wolf's prayer.
Lines from an old song come unbidden;
they're troubling me today:

See there those strangers comin'
See them there, those you don't know
See there the strangers comin'
lookin' quick and talkin' low
You don't live here anymore
you soon will have to go...

Room

Those things had trapped us. Later they signaled
each other from designated piles: Save/Donate/Trash.
Telepathic somehow, heap called out to heap.
Gone, but only just—we could still envision those
ousted items: petrified rollers and paint pans,
cans of shellac. Two chairs (seats burst)
astride a steamer trunk. The way the 30's toilet tank had
wooed the Persian jardinière. How a pair of bicycles nuzzled
by the built-in cupboard. What else was there?
Dibber. Sickle craving an edge. Hay rake
bereft of tines, hiding among the croquet mallets.
One brick. A trio of trowels we rated good, better, best.
Twine possessed of Gordian Knot, and the
topless table: a pedestal poised on lion paws,
suggestive of a sphinx.

Elsewhere, bed linens mixed with drop cloths and a
tan Stetson sat atop them. Boxes (contents unknown)
partnered buckets of nails. A folding screen we shifted
revealed a clear corner.

We swept. Tore down drapes—July broke in with
clarion bursts. Freshly viewed, the space
altered: the ceiling rose and the walls
stood back. The mopped floor glowed,
suggesting flow.

Glass commanded, and the final
window (crystal after cleaning) yielded up a
catbird nest whose comfort rode on thorny canes, where we
perceived—snug in the weave—an intricate riddle.
Empty or full? The cup bejeweled with
three fallen blackberries.

The News

We hadn't thought to meet the messenger
during rush hour, but then, why not?

We mean this man who confronts the
crowd pouring down this stairwell,
where they'll catch the L train east or west,
to ride where they must. No rider he, but the boulder the
cascade swerves in waves—to the left,
everyone to the left, since he hugs the stair rail.
He has climbed two steps, half standing and
half sunk, gaze fixed on the ascent. The eyes
in his face rimmed with vermilion, yes, we must use that
word, it betokens no ordinary red, but seems the blood
of the man risen to ring his stare and confound us.
His look says he cannot be thwarted, that
fiends have schooled him, abandoned him underground
to climb what cannot be surmounted, but that he
must, or he will be flogged, racked and skewered.

Dressed entirely in newspapers, he rustles as he moves.
No cloth visible, no skin, except that of his face
and hands—hands he's locked upon the bannister
millions have touched. Perhaps this connection
animates him, generates headlines from his crackle.
He is his own tailor and he fashions for us
the news, as we swerve and break where he clings,
nearly drowning in our flood. He brings the stories we
fear, he has come a long way,
striving to rise.

Books In A Dumpster

One foot on the step rail,
I heft my
weight, clutching the stained side.
Peer down,
confronted by castaways.

Outside the library,
afternoon spent and
book sale finished,
there came the hurling.

Your flutter-fall
gave rise to doleful mountain:
first layer beneath second,
second interred below
third—batch upon batch
till culling ended.

No one to pluck you out,
old darlings.
No shock since binding
as blithering as this.
Wrenched if not bent before.
Rent if not torn earlier.
Like game, inert save when a
breeze rifles pages
revealing secret wounds:
ink blots, marginalia.

This plot doesn't fall between
covers, my friends, and the
characters taking stage
confound.
You templed text entire as noun
but ah! text leapt to verb.

All worlds in time must come
to tilt, and their centuries prove unwieldy.
Yet still amazed, this reader
gazes down
afraid.

Song Of Sleeping Rough

Look. Now heaven's vault arcs higher,
the scrutiny of stars burn colder.
Concrete's kiss breeds a nightly affliction.
Feel the hands of the wind grow bolder.

Rent! The rent rose up like mountains beheld,
and the bills attained blaze and tail,
orbiting till you were dazzled then downed.
Instructions await you in braille.

Read. Get what a park bench says through
obscenities carved and the catch of splinters.
Predictions encrypted in gouged initials of
needs for cardboard and foil in winter.

Can you make them out? Do they recall
childhood's tent? Back when camping spelled
an idyll among the murmurous trees.
What price for the lone birch felled

and dry, kindled by build to ferry you far?
Smoke would provide the kindly tide, sparks
the steadfast compass, flames the feast against
sleeplessness and the ever-hungering dark.

III. Crossroads

After Reading Stories By Chekhov

No gaunt horse awaits the lash
from surly peasant to convey
the timid surveyor through frigid
miles to where the numb farm waits.

Not Moscow, this, not Mironitski, nor
Russia, even. But wild flakes quicken
and leap. Trees stand stricken; heart of
mercury lies pinned by a stake of ice.

And you, my love, where are you,
eternal, unmarried Manetchka,
train-ridden, two-timing Agatha who
yearns for a man who despises women?

And you, my love, where are you
withheld and withholding Byelinkoff,
the nameless (till later) Lushkoff,
hostage to vodka, redeemed by a cook?

By city windows I muse, from
hawk's height stare three stories
down. What mysteries you've ignited.
What inn fires after endless snow!

The West Bedroom

They bet me I couldn't stay a week in the

mauve room that faced west. The wallpaper's
silvery branches heating or chilling in

changes of light. Whether they
blossomed was up to the ghost. (I recalled

they'd said she). The lamps appeared to
dim at times, the furniture to crouch.

I waited; she didn't deign to show me she had
noticed. I strained towards what she'd say or do—

she never did. Told myself that recurrent
rustling was mice, but circumvented her

mirror from sunset to sunrise. No, no, I
would never survive myself glimpsed in

glassy depths, attired in moiré dress, the
scent of violets abrupt on the air. My hand

ceaseless with her silver-backed brush, my
face stunned. And my shock and my

inheritance her electric wealth of hair

Two Views From The Cabin Window At Platte Clove

I. Interior

This gloom of the kind that Poe dubbed "sable."
I lie undisturbed and delighted, stretched
upon single bed in a room memory will fetch
faithfully for me (years hence) by livid cables

of lightning. Darkest-of-dark varnish upon
grooved boards ensure my solitary surround.
Pale chest of drawers and side chair astounded
by their own hues when the flashes, lordly, come

to transport me like a lover's touch from one
realm to another. Each furthers me from myself,
I slough off shaming histories, accrue a wealth of
nothingness so heady I feel drunk or undone.

In thunder I lie, beneath wiles of a sheet that—Bang!
shows peaks of meringue in the flash, or moonscape.
My eyes, like an alien's, silvered from the uptake,
upon my tongue, the storm's sulphurous tang.

II. Exterior

The hour commands that The Unknown Artist pencil
in silverpoint what sight conceives. This means
the rain, of course, the quickening falls that teem
this night of forces converging. Truthful and tensile,

these dislocated trees. One wants to believe their roots
hold, but they cavort as only trees of inspiration can.
Draw. Keep drawing, whoever you are. Innis and Durand,
Cole and Church and who knows else are in cahoots.

Tonight the scenes they love are striped as moose maple,
as startling as birch—that lovely bride. The pliant dark,
lit up, bends time and space; this red cabin represents my ark.
I am its single creature. The old boarding house? Incapable,

roof in ruins. The loggers who came for timber? Gone.
The forest fires? Passing. The quarrymen? Under stones
of their own. The farmers? Glaciers plowed here. Blown
leaves whip by. One gives the glass a kiss, the song

it sings—when lifting off—a secret. Preserve, I tell
The Unknown Artist, and he or she intuits I mean "draw."
And knows the place to be protected. By varied spells
legal and romantic. By legacy. By what the painters saw.

To An Iron Headboard
Found In The Plattekill

More startling than the foundry was life mid-stream.
From a house folded like paper then torn, flood left you
submerged to speak with stones perfecting their
rounds. When I broke in on your Plattekill dream

you had already lain in water (ever refreshed),
how many years? Patina russet as hairs in a fox pelt,
not a trace of paint left, but each of your ornate
flowers intact, no worse for having been threshed

through the current's mill, ground by seasonal
cycles as though you were grain. You are. Just a
single grain of endeavor. Once new. Once sentinel over
sleep, insomnia, sex. Observing a winding frieze

of domestic scenes. Coffee-crested, that flood, bold
the way it bore you away—a lover, taken. Which did
you prefer? The couples or the stones? Parted from
bedframe, still you long to support a load, to uphold

in air or water. At the foundry, they whorled your
ends inward, formed a lyre. How could they know you'd
dock at last in mud, cast up? Scroll-ends of iron-fancy
sunk near woodland ferns. Your thin bars strung for

the finder, your music chromatic and lost.

A Single Birch At Day's End

Slender birch beckons from among somber firs.
She sways; where her arms join her ecstatic body

dark marks, triangular, mimic the mountains
beyond. Ranges unexplored despite your plans.

Sunset. The struck birch strikes in turn the
optic nerve: a torch carried to the

cave where conscience hides, as questions
rack spirit and shake body for reply.

Sunset. Sky-fires burning towards your heart.
You know longing is a blue canoe; you know the

restless waters of the eye rise and sweep all
chance away before you've even cried.

July 17th

I.

How not to grasp at the transitory tonight when
lightning takes such liberties with our eyes, we

drive up the hill to watch the spectacle, rushing
so as not to miss what promises to be gesture after

gesture of electrical genius? It began tamely,
heat lightning, nothing strange about those

jittery glimpses that played predictably, rife with
delay and drunk on repetition, yet soon invention

ruled. Who was it, then, who sent the signal?
Which lime-white entity seeks to bend horizon,

inhale and exhale clouds? Rogue shapes arrive, not
ones we recognize. They ride the landscape's undulant

curves in stealth, devoid of thunder. Pressing
orchestral silence upon us. Sullen between

strikes, they segue into wars seen from afar, disasters
occluded by distance, enacted in stuttering dark. The

wounds don't stop: dying is everywhere sustained.
These bolts say so. Their voltage seems not to care to

be accompanied at all, but to climb silence monkey-
wise, demonic. Which wars? Trojan, we guess, since

mythic clout rides here in force, but then come others
slinking in, transforming us to generals on a hill removed

from battle. The fights progress, as does the illusion we'll
win this one. But this clash, pyro-teching, recalls Vietnam.

Over there, fresher conflicts draw closer by the second.
Lurid views. We cannot hold them long—but history can.

II.

Was it wind? The way the moon fell through a slit from
where she spied? Now brusque angels duel, gilt letters

fall from the Book Of Crooked. An eland's horn
jousts a sudden tower. Here's a kiss from someone's past

come hissing to haunt. Unpaid debts crackle while
money burns in balls. Blue orchard of x-rayed apples says

we'll not forget this night (*ever, ever,* twin strokes
scrawl on slate). Extending neck for miles, a swan courts—

with ravaged curve—star-hordes of the hidden galaxy.
We must go home, passing crossroads into infinity.

The Hawthorns

Breaking through at every step, I'm winded
when I reach the summit.   Twilight.
Blue surround of blended vistas.

Hard to breathe easy. This kind of cold injects a
sting, and goads me on with marble touch.
Best not to stand still. Two trees await—

they've not closed yet, won't embrace for a few
years more. The gap between them beckons,
tells me if I brave the narrows,

I will be remade.   Such is their blossomed

power, potent in December, branches laden with a
thousand - weight of flakes. Their blooms pierced,
borne on a black fretwork of thorns.

Two trees. How they strive, mesmerized by
their own reach. Petition the seasons to unite
them, dare and endure the blank field.

What will transpire within that space if I am
held but not torn, emerge coroneted by snow
sudden wind shook down, and

who shall I be in my brief reign, how
far my wanderings then?

Whitepark Bay, Northern Ireland

It is said of this place that the sand sings,
that the grains under stress of your steps
will give voice. You cannot—where mingling

coast and sea mate—discern what's said.
But farther back from tidal dalliance and
plovers' complaints, the whispers of the dead

distill to clarity. And the living? The living
emit their tiny hurrahs. In between lie the
shy almosts, the not-yets softly forgiving

inattention. Blended together, the triad
forge their desires; your footsteps kindle their
choir. In the tumult of tumble-and-slide, glad

to rub, they sing with anguished kindness.
Their song refines them: fiercest, gentlest yet.
Music that summons the sudden taste of salt.
Thrill, as when the blindfold slips the blinded.

Highland (with borrowings from Scots)

Thistle on the hill. Purple too, the evening cloud.
The sunrise orange, the fields orange, the window glass
licked orange then gold, licked clear as air again.

You can, you canna know of my love for you,
save when the grass greens, when the whitethroat
wheedles seven syllables. Seven.
You can, you canna know of my love for you, save when the
wind blows, and serviceberry leaves comb the breeze.

Wicked the thistle, you canna be gallus. Aloof royal.
   No touching.
Thwarts the picker. Let's smell it, though. Have hue
   intoxicate.
Let's run while the deer watch. The twosome together.
The twasame thegither. 'Tis the time of pairs. The deer,
orange and gold.

You can, you canna know of my love for you, save when the
stones wear down. When the owl floats twinned inside her
ghost. Moon-gilt, the mouse in the talon. You can,
you canna know how lang I've loved. The years run forth
and back, vertical as the harp, horizontal as the seas.

I've a brown eye and a grey eye for you; I've a green eye
and an eye of blue to cherish sight of you.
You can, you canna see how long my love exceedan lasts
save by the way the spider weaves and by the willows'
green-stitching. By the geese returned—the twosome together,
   the twasame thegither.

Razor-whist, those thistle leaves, but no bee resists the blossom,
no goldfinch shuns the white-spun when purple's fled.
So shall we be to one another as time hones us on an edge.
We slicken with a wish to clasp what dwindles yet
what richens. The twasame thegither. Feathers on wind,
we skim clouds of evening. Gold a rim
we'll reach and vault. Gone.

The Mouse

Cold has come, its emissary the mouse
entering our kitchen. Out and about for crumbs,
even as we eat. Tiny flame, flickering
here, there.

*

Remember last time? Herald Square: you sat in the
circle of a planter, turning a berry as if tracking
famine's progress on the globe, or
holding up a ruby for the poor to admire.
No one else saw you; I was on my way to buy parsley,
to see a friend, or perhaps to sign significant papers.
And spotted you beneath leaves like mimics of your ears,
the round of the planter like the
world that can neither keep you in nor out.
  There you sat, little Jet Eyes,
          nestling one curve to another.

Mouse, I thought, marveling. *Monster,* you thought,
but didn't flinch, jaded by the giants
crowding your Upper World. Ten feet away, the
yellow slur of speeding taxis. Closer in, the crush
of shopping bags, buffeting briefcases.
Mouths stretched wide, the
weeping children passed, imprisoned in strollers,
as cell phones rang against the two/four time of feet.
  Everywhere,
hands held phones that here and there were raised
to ward off others' words, and a siege of sirens.

Bold! You distain dark, patter about in full view.
Casual. Winsomely teasing us
towards adoption. You ignore the trap with its Gorgonzola;
we abandon our feud and
name you, and as if you sensed our
tolerance growing, you venture tonight
near the toe of my shoe.
No one moves; I know you are saying there's
nothing you haven't sampled
of blue-foot and chanterelle, of olive and
Saltine. You have crossed the ladle's bridge to sip
carrot-ginger soup, stored in your pantry
pilfered lentils to lie with wild seeds. You know the
blueberry bears the mark of a star
folklore claims it fell from. You dislike cinnamon, but
recall the nest of the Phoenix includes it, accept it
therefore, baked into a bun. Corn you worship as true gold,
consider bacon fine seduction.
Attuned to when pear, when popcorn
falls, you have attended countless performances,
trekked between wine and blood
(O, cycle of tables! Art & rebellion!).

And you say (without sound, without movement)
that—should the banquet be withdrawn—
you would eat again of the candle,
bar of soap or shoelace, even the photograph, if necessary,
fueling yourself for one more day
on bride and groom
poised smiling before their wedding cake.

Twice

Note: Monarch butterflies migrate to Mexico in winter,
where they cluster by the thousands in pines and oyamel firs.

December. I open a drawer to find a bra
rearranged.   Look what marquetry awaits:
how mouse inlays with butterfly. One cup is
stuffed with milkweed silk—
milkweed that drew to its mauve stars
the monarchs to hang forgetful,
when fragrance claimed all.
What cupped one breast now brims with
filaments chosen for the mouse's nest.   Breast, rest,
some rhyme insists, then tucks itself away.
I close my eyes, see oyamel firs massed in amber.
The butterflies migrated, but the mouse must stay.

An icicle drops from the eaves as I imagine the mouse,
bedded in luxury even satin cannot best. A tiny yawn,
then two dark seeds amid the white fluff vanish.
Ever inward, sleep's plummet, ever outward
the dream-flow—how far the drift through
fields? Or did the mouse stay home?

*

Home, I say, but mine lies split between two places.
Upon return, I find within the same drawer a second nest,
of batting this time, extracted bit by bit from a chair.
A whisper—Burns, no doubt, his burr
distinct in my ear: "*Monie a weary nibble.*"
Aye, friend, and wound into the ivory hue of old cotton,

veins of blue, making the nest resemble mottled cheese.
I'd not deduce its source till spring, when through a
towel unfolded, I viewed my room through
ragged peephole, stunned by the
intimate glimpse. Blue, the threads of recall.
swift on the spool of shame. My hands. Their
double theft of steadfast labors. Warp and weft
the tiny weaver wove against the cold.
"Best laid schemes," murmurs Burns, *"best laid schemes."*

Sloppy And Mephisto

No hoof, no horse. So says the old adage.
To which I'll add: No roof, no house.
Let the curtain rise, let the players enter
to enact their little drama
on a May day dry and cool and sunny.

Nameless, they pull themselves through
the roof's trap door,
first the panther, then the clown,
for a casual cigarette, and a careful
look around. They walk perimeters,
push aside a branch of mulberry tree,

bounce up and down with caution
to see if the roof is sound and will take
their weight when rolls of roofing, ropes,
and buckets of tar are added.
They sniff the air, satisfied,
disappear below, and when I look out later
all has been assembled; Mephisto works
stripped to the waist. Sloppy watches.

Mephisto? How could it be other, this lithe
and muscled man, café au lait colored,
with black eyes and grizzled mane? But if you
doubt my christening, know he wields
a torch, flame tip flaring on a long rod
with which he melts the seams together.

And Sloppy? That's easy.
Loose-jointed, he lounges against the chimney,
someone's errant nephew, his clothes permanently askew.
Smoking cigarettes with impunity
in the kingdom of flammables. And Mephisto
lets him, Mephisto laughs and curses him, too,
dancing a rooster's dance with his boots
over the freshly torched seams. He times it so he won't
burn, nor disgrace the work of his torch.
His torch is a woman, a dangerous woman
whom he pleases and partners in a dance.

Hand in glove, feather on bird,
a man at one with his work is sleek.
He's all of a piece, elegant,
and makes you believe in the world.
You could watch all day the roofing trade
as danced by Mephisto.
Romance! Passion! Danger!
Sloppy lights another cigarette. Mephisto
tangos by, lost in a series of fresh steps.

He finishes, looks about his open air,
Brooklyn ballroom. A small rooftop in
Williamsburg, a view down on someone's garden.
A woman works there, pruning a shrub.
He appraises her, grins wickedly,
calls softly down: "Hey, you want a roofer?"
Five starlings flick over his head.
He turns to Sloppy, bows, says something
mocking. Strides to the open trap,
drops through like a shot.

Alone, Sloppy slops,
an extravagant snail trailing silver.
Section by section he claims the roof
and at last he mops the chimney
which leans a little, and which
becomes his silent, silver overseer.
A cigarette now. He contemplates
this god of the roof, then suddenly, urgently packs up.
Everything goes down anyhow, the trap door
crashes on his head.

*

Evening. The luminous stage lies empty.
Along the edge, Sloppy's hallmark: a ragged row of drips.
Like a cake clumsily iced—but lasting;
I shall have to look at it for years.
A reminder of how work finds us,
and how we find work:
as a furrow of boredom, a primer for pain
or as divine assignation.

Sloppy, I wish you well.
Mephisto, I send my compliments.

A Day Of Thaw, Brooklyn

We passed the tied spaniel, tongue lolling in dog
laughter, drew near the kid with dirty snowball.
"Beep, beep!" he cried politely, waving us aside.

Out of his zone, we pressed on, fixated by a guy
nesting in the pocket of his girlfriend's coat. He withdrew
his hand, put it back, while a rooftop mockingbird sang

some variant of "Nice Work If You Can Get It."
The gutter offered a red rag paired with stale bagel,
jigged by a pigeon whose houndstooth wings

snagged our sight. Small dazzle, that interlock of
black and white. The sidewalk glinted. Or was it winking?
A-gleam, whatever the mode, and a wheel-chaired

someone went smartly by, hair astray and scarf
heraldic. Everyone, we love you. Saints and scoundrels,
let's strut. Clear your throats and shuck patience,

sing loudly of what quickens. Sing to startle! Wake up
these Bradford pears—let's hasten our ornamentals.
We ask that the next snow be strictly of petals.

A Mockingbird In Williamsburg

Let me sing like the mockingbird
I listen to as I write,
his clarity broadcast upon
morning stirred by cool air
mingling nascent greens
the eye might recognize:
hues heralding maple and cherry,
those of oak, of sweet gum and
sycamore and locust, too,
go on, keep going, the mocker sings
list, list them all, improvise
and soliloquize
gingko and beech (I continue)
tra la la tree! the mocker interjects,
mimosa, princess tree, I counter.
Paulownia! he whistles, *tomentosa!*
at no loss with botanical Latin
and he gives it a couple of bars.
Me Tree! he peals, ornament at the top.
Geisha Song! he trills, fanning then
shutting wings and tail,
faking a swoon before he flitters up
like ash on the bosom of heat, oh
I have lost my trees
in a forest inside his creation—
mojito, he carols drunkenly, *juniper, juniper,*
sloe gin! Whoever listens
will turn giddy with
potential, feel sleek and silk-lined,

adrift on the River of Elixir.
Let me sing with his tongue and
he with mine, let my silence
continue his presence in silence,
let me grant him time
until he would burst forth again.
Let me hear him always in this world,
and when I have flown.

Copper Beech, Chatham Rural Cemetery

Giant, who birthed you, monument who deprives
us of speech? Dwarfing obelisks and other trees,
you stretch and gesture, elephantine. To have thrived
long, to rise as though you stood when the world began

sparks awe we honor by walking rings around you,
as if we generated with those circles something eternal
ourselves. The day (grey when we got here) burns blue,
as flawless and as clear as the wish to move among stones,

vitally alive and near to all these unknown who beckon
mutely with names and dates, and by the stonecutter's art
delight and sober us by turns. Tiny, wily split seconds
fall from our lives and hide in the grass among violets.

After we've marveled over our many and long-gentled kin,
we return to stand beneath you and gaze up. Leaf upon leaf,
three centuries stir and play. Furred haloes edge fresh skin.
Light lifts us up to set us among the layered, translucent reds.

The Gift

in memory of Eve Crane, British expert on World's bees

Someone gave you a swarm.
You had married in wartime
when the rationing of sugar
held to meager measures,

the giver not guessing his gift
would generate such wealth.
Equations solved at the
university joined with your

masters in quantum mechanics.
Nuclear physics doctorate next,
then bride and bailiwick took wing.
Numbers were your thing and

bees held numbers' essence.
One might call you Queen in her
keep of One, who went out to greet
the workers' thousands,

your mind capacious, your soul the ample skep.

Far afield, by dog sled and dugout
you went, collecting beekeeping ways
of cultures for preservation. Savoring then
setting in print the ancient methods.

International bee authority, researcher,
archivist, author, historian—prolific,
those pollinations. Even as days flitted,
you willed them to multiply,
tasting and tasting of the honey,

dying at ninety-five.

Curating At 10 p.m.

Pileated woodpecker? Prehistoric.
So shy I couldn't install him.
I tried to fasten the swags of his flight;
he flew through a hole in memory.

At twilight, an Inca figure traveled the road.

The moon is a Roman coin, dented by her
current phase. I need to quit, to breathe
deeply and relax, but my mind keeps
cataloguing. Where's peace? Where's the case
for enclosing cricket song? Is that starlight

beading like solder on the run of
Roaring Brook, while the moon (smelted now)
pours out smoothly on the sills?
Every windowpane has assumed
Venetian origin: they are thinnest of thin,
seeded and intact.

These tree shadows—what period are they?
Tokugawa, perhaps? The room yields matte and
lacquer creatures, wrought by tricks of light.
A changing exhibition guided by the
night, secret and sacred in the late hours.

What keeps me awake is the newborn
calf discovered this morning.
Where to archive the feel of how it sucked
my fingers? Ancient, the pull of the mouth

thrilling nerves up my arm, the
sensation sounding my heart
with one-day-old tongue.

Then I Will Go Out

for Cynthia Artin

Then I will go out to the Fortune irises, bowing
(in mind's eye) and drawing near the group to
stop and softly say, *How are you, Glorious Ones?*

And they, robed in purple and white with signals of yellow,
tasting the currents of air and bees' inquiry-kiss
and the moistures of morning, will greet me with silence

though in no way hostile, simply the distillation of how
they can perfectly be (swaying perhaps) in place
while the spider of black and gold makes construct

as silken as they, as arresting, in the foliage beneath their
heads, and a symphony emanates for the observer,
music that unfurled when they did and that

blooms' demise doesn't finish: something of the violet
veining through the white (draw close and you'll confirm
that this is so) runs on beyond the end of bloom to hours

that come as summer lightning does to strike and
strike, igniting in the senses fever
one seeks not to throw off but be taken by.

Photographer And Spring Peeper

for Tom Artin

I opened the door as gently as I could to photograph the peeper from the other side. It was dark, and unfortunately shooting that way, I couldn't brace the camera, so the photo isn't sharp (1/2 second exposure, hand-held). The second after I took the picture, the little fellow hopped off the pane of the door, now open to the room. Luckily, he landed on the Hamburg stool, which I was able cautiously to lift and carry to return him to the great outdoors.

*

I am suction and song. Darkness drew me, then light, what I clung to swung, some Greatness loomed—I leapt. My landing did not keep the stillness sought; some buoyance claimed me, sudden as the rush to sing. I want (oh, my tribe) to voice that pond I glimpsed, of shapes strange, of depth bewildering, in spots bejeweled, in others, dimmed. The water there made mimic of the air, the place pure Threat and Marvel. I have come home. Let us sing a chorus (I will lead) to celebrate this telling, before we bell the woods with Love's wet name.

The Bee

Working among flowers, I came upon a
bee who seemed oblivious, and struck me
either as drowsing or dying.

A bumblebee, face over-powdered
with pollen. And wanting to step where I
could finish my task, I fondled it out of the

mallow with gloved fingers, and treading the
texture of my roughened glove, this bee ascended
towards my wrist as if on a circular stair and

sleepwalking. Into the somnolent whorl I was
drawn, to make rounds wherever the call.
Dosed with elixirs and focused as a fanatic.

What a purposeful dream! I doubt I'd ever have
waked, but for a touch on my vein of
one jet foot. Hyper-light. Velcro-electric.

My blue vein a path the bee set one foot on,
testing the way before it thought to cross.
I offered my left hand glove for taking,

gazing upon the pollen-dusted face that
seemed sleepy, endearing somehow, and like
someone I knew. Into another mallow I palmed it,

moment and movement both honeyed.
There, lover clasped the beloved,
rapturous and private. I could not turn away.

Sleeping In The Bed
of the One Hundred And One
Year Old Woman

On a raised platform,
in simplicity, joinery fitted
together like lovers
by Nakashima the woodworker
who also lived long,

we lie, holding hands

I recall a note Bernarda
once wrote when we
stayed overnight five years ago
I regret to say I
no longer iron any sheets

outside in the small black pond
spring peepers sing
blending voices into a single
silver pencil, outlining
trees, moon, stars,
filling the pale magnolia's cups
to let them brim or
shatter, limning the
swamp's subtle waters
that tickle the
crisscross of fallen sticks

nothing can hold forever

not the master craftsman's skill,
not Bernarda's hand drawing
nor that same hand ironing,
pressing to perfect cotton's
smell and feel and
not the magnolia towering
within the song of praise
yes yes yes sing the peepers
loudly, to refute time,
and in their melt I move to kiss you

grant us long life, I ask of no one,
or of gods never sought before
who hold the bed aloft
an inch or two above the platform

(deep in our embrace
we don't feel them swaying)
yes yes yes sing the peepers
hypnotic, in love themselves,
they seal us and stamp us in silver,
float us down the creek to sleep
on the bed made tight as a
puzzle and finished as
fine as silk

Bernarda is watching from the moon,
the gods carry us through till dawn
those nameless ones,
who listen when possible,
give what they can

NOTES

"Yakshi With A Love Letter In Her Hand": Many statues of yakshi exist, but this particular one, circa 11th or 12th century, is in the collection of the Herbert F. Johnson Museum Of Art, Ithaca, NY.

"Elderflower In Bloom": The made up word "umbrels" is intended as a bridge between the real ones of "umbel" and "umbrella."

"Foreclosure": The lines of the "old song" are of my own invention.

"Love Poem To A Maple Leaf In The Ouleout": The Ouleout Creek runs through Delaware County, New York. According to one source, the name is said to mean "rapid waters" in the language of the indigenous peoples of the area. Some stretches allow for whitewater canoeing.

"Twice": The italicized comments of Robert Burns are drawn from his poem "To A Mouse, On Turning Her Up in her Nest with the Plough, November, 1785."

"Sleeping Rough": U.K. slang referring to the condition of being homeless, or to be sleeping uncomfortably, outside and without shelter. Cardboard and foil are sought after materials for the warmth they generate.

"Two Views From The Cabin Window At Platte Clove": Plattekill Falls and the cabin mentioned are located at the top of Platte Clove. Areas of the Catskills, including some of the Cloves, were venerated by the Hudson River School painters and inspired their paintings.

80

"Highland (With Borrowings From Scots)"
canna (cannot)
gallus (wicked)
twasame (twosome) & thegither (together)
lang (long)
exceedan (exceeding)
razor-whist – invented, to describe thistle leaves

"Photographer And Spring Peeper": The first stanza of the poem is found, taken from an e-mail I received from Tom Artin, who sent me an image of the frog and his account of photographing it.

"Sleeping In The Bed Of The One Hundred And One Year Old Woman": The woman named in the poem is Bernarda Shahn, painter and illustrator, who lived in Roosevelt, NJ. George Nakashima, an American woodworker, architect, and furniture maker, constructed the second story of the Shahns' house, and built much of the furniture within it.